To Jennifer
and
Mark

Edited by Anna H. Centola and Gary Centola

TABLE OF CONTENTS

This book was written for all those guitarists who have tried all the standard, conventional methods for learning how to read music yet are still unable to master this seemingly difficult task.

After years of research, I have derived a simple, straightfoward, yet totally effective method which will have you reading music easily and enjoyably in just a short period of time.

Ron Centola

SPECIAL FEATURES

1) Important points are in **bold print.**

2) The staffs are specially coded so that you are given the string and fret position of each line and space of the staff on the neck of the guitar.

3) The names of the lines and spaces are also coded in the staff.

4) Beat signs are placed on the music so that you know where to stop and count.

5) Songs are presented in a step-by-step, easy-to-follow method.

6) You are given plenty of practice with familiar tunes.

7) Songs are written in large, easy to read notes.

LIST OF SONGS

GUITAR DIAGRAM

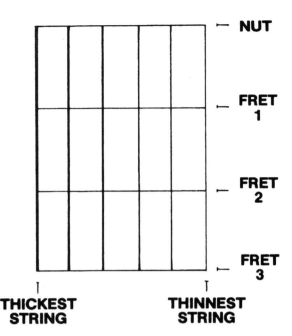

NUT

FRET 1

FRET 2

FRET 3

This diagram will be used throughout the book to show finger positions on the guitar.

THICKEST STRING

THINNEST STRING

HOW TO READ FINGER POSITIONS ON THE GUITAR DIAGRAM

○ indicates finger placed on guitar. The number in the circle would be the number of the finger used on your hand.

② indicates the **2nd finger** on **String 3, Fret 2.**

③ indicates the **3rd finger** on **String 5, Fret 3.**

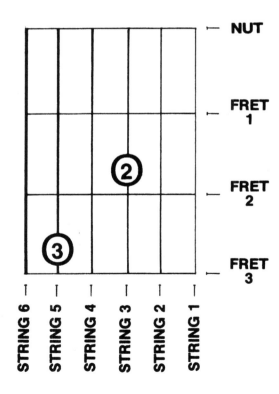

NUT

FRET 1

FRET 2

FRET 3

STRING 6 STRING 5 STRING 4 STRING 3 STRING 2 STRING 1

BASIC ELEMENTS OF MUSIC

Most of the elements of music that you will need to know will be learned while actually playing the guitar. Here are some things you should be familiar with to start.

The Staff

1) Music for the guitar as well as any other instrument, will be placed on a standard **staff** which consists of **5 lines** and **4 spaces.**

A. 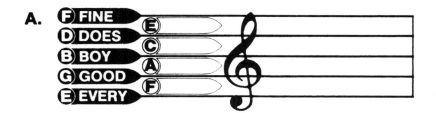   These lines **are not** the **strings** of **the guitar.**

B. A way to remember the lines of the staff is by using the sentence **Every Good Boy Does Fine**. The first letter of each word indicates the name of the line. The spaces may be remembered easily since they spell **"FACE"**.

2)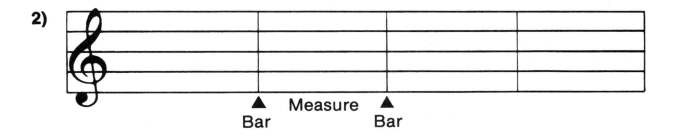

A. The **bars** are a way of dividing the staff into segments called measures. **The measure is the space between two bars.**

3)

G Clef

This is a **G Clef.** All music written for the guitar will be preceded by this clef sign.

Time Signatures

4)

A. The G Clef will be found at the beginning of each line.

B. The **time signature** will be found at the **beginning of the song,** next to the G Clef. It is NOT found on the following lines of the song.

C.

◀ This number indicates there are **4 beats** to **a measure.**

◀ This number indicates the **type of note** that **receives one beat.** (A quarter note receives one beat in all the above time signatures.)

D. A beat is a measure of time in music. **One beat** is **equal** to the **down, up** tap of your foot.

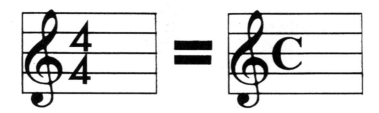

Most songs are written
in ⁴⁄₄ time.
a C is often
used instead of ⁴⁄₄.

Since ⁴⁄₄ is the most common
time used, the meaning,
however, is the same.

Remembering The Names Of Notes

A. Notes are a way of communicating the musical language, as words are a way of communicating spoken language. You will learn to translate the notes from the musical staff and apply them to the guitar.

B. The note is composed of two parts; the ball and the stem.

◀ **BALL**

◀ **STEM**

C. The note takes the name of the line or space of the staff upon which the ball of the note is placed.

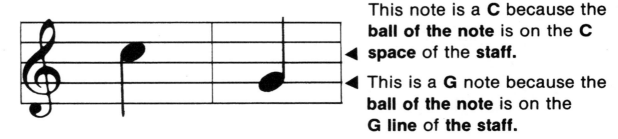

This note is a **C** because the **ball of the note** is on the **C space** of the **staff.**

This is a **G** note because the **ball of the note** is on the **G line** of the **staff.**

D. It doesn't matter which way the stem of the note is going. The direction of the stem does not affect the name of the note.

Musical Alphabet

The musical alphabet is limited to 7 letters. A,B,C,D,E,F, and G. (The musical alphabet repeats itself for a greater variation in notes.) A,B,C,D,E,F,G,A,B,C, etc.

1) The **key** to the **note's position** on the **neck of the guitar** is the **ball of the note.**

2) Where the **ball of the note** is placed **on the staff determines** where its **position** is **on the neck** of the **guitar.**

3) We have coded the beginning of the staff to show you where the note is placed on the neck of the guitar. The **Guitar Position Guide** shows the string and fret position of the lines and spaces of the staff.

EXAMPLE

GUITAR POSITION GUIDE

The balls of all these notes are on the **F line of the staff** and are all played on **String 1 - Fret 1.** (As shown on the Guitar Position Guide.)

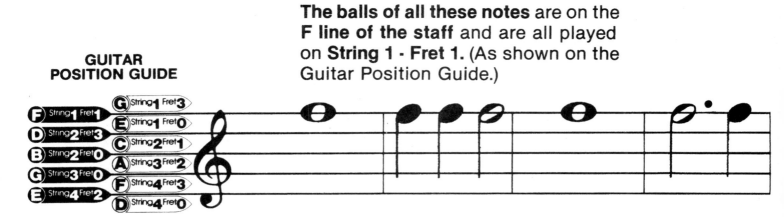

All of the above notes are played on **String 1 - Fret 1.** Remember the only important factor to consider is where the ball of the note is. The fact that a note has a different shape or may be solid or hollow should not concern you. The various notes look different because of their beat value. This will be discussed in detail in the next section of this book.

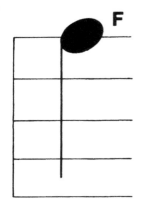

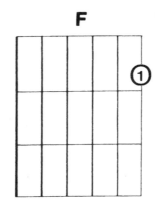

This is the guitar position of the F notes. Remember you should be using your **1st finger** because you are on **Fret 1.**

GUITAR POSITION GUIDE

▲ ▲

All of the above notes are on the **C space of the staff.** Their position on the guitar is on **String 2, Fret 1.**

All of the above notes are on the **G line of the staff.** Their position on the guitar is on **String 3, Open.**

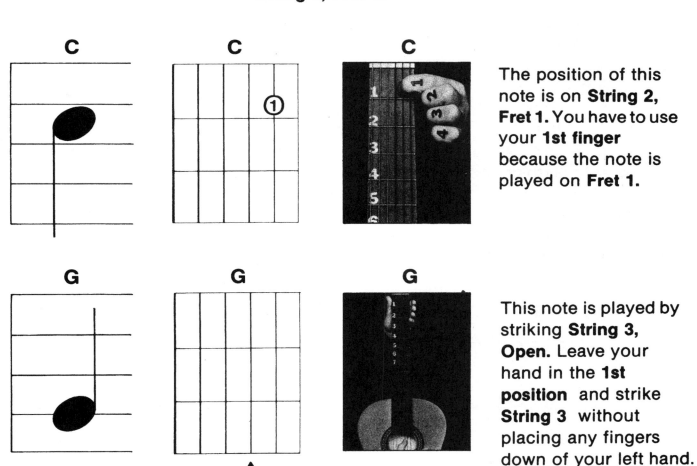

The position of this note is on **String 2, Fret 1.** You have to use your **1st finger** because the note is played on **Fret 1.**

Strike This String

This note is played by striking **String 3, Open.** Leave your hand in the **1st position** and strike **String 3** without placing any fingers down of your left hand.

Making Things Simple

Below is a chart showing the relationship between the notes, the staff, and their position on the guitar.

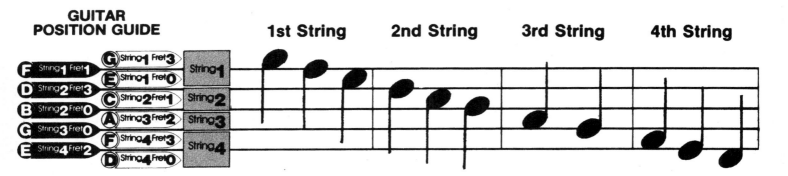

The notes and their positions on the guitar are represented in this chart of the four strings. First you will learn the first four strings, then you will learn the notes and their positions for the fifth and sixth strings.

Memorize

It is easier to learn the note positions once you realize that the line or space of the staff that the ball of the note rests upon will tell you where to play the note on the guitar. Example: Anytime the **ball of the note** is on the **F line of the staff** the **note is played** on **String 1, Fret 1**. Anytime the **ball of the note** is on the **A space of the staff** the note is played on **String 3, Fret 2**.

Student Notes

A beat is a regular and rhythmical unit of time.

How Much Time Is A Beat?

A beat takes the amount of time it takes to tap your foot. The down, up motion of your foot will constitute one beat.

How Fast Is A Beat?

The speed depends on the tempo or speed of the song you are playing. In a slow song the tap of your foot or the speed of a beat is slower than in a fast song.

The Visible Beat

It is the **way the note looks,** not its position on the staff, **that determines its beat value.** In other words, the form of the note tells you how many beats it receives. The three note forms that we will begin with are the whole note, the half note, and the quarter note.

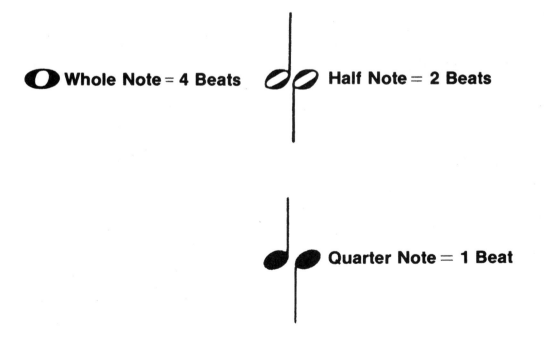

Whole Note = 4 Beats   **Half Note = 2 Beats**

Quarter Note = 1 Beat

The Invisible Beat

The striking of the whole note, half note, or quarter note is one beat. Therefore, striking the whole note takes one of the four beats the note is actually worth. Striking the half note takes one of the two beats the note is actually worth. Striking the quarter note takes one beat or the entire value of the note. (Further explanation and diagrams are on the following page.)

The Beat

A beat is a duration of time. In this book each beat will be represented by the symbol. Each symbol will represent 1 beat or 1 tap (the down, up motion) of your foot. This symbol will be used to remind you to give each note its correct beat value.

How Does The System Work?

A. **O** Whole Note= 4 beats, the whole note is followed by. Striking the note is the first beat. No beat symbol is needed above the note itself. The three beat symbols after the whole note are there to remind you to count or tap three beats after you play the note. **Remember you strike the note only once, the remaining three beats are counted or tapped.**

B. Half Note= 2 beats, the half note is followed by one symbol. Striking the half note is the first beat. The beat symbol is there to remind you to wait one beat after you strike the note so it receives its full two beat value.

C. Quarter Note = 1 beat. Since quarter notes are worth one beat, no beat symbols will be needed. **Striking the note equals one beat.** How to play these notes will be discussed on the following pages.

NOTE VALUES AND COUNTING

Notes take on different forms because their note or beat values are different. You must know how to count note values if you are going to read music. Let us begin with the three basic notes: The whole note, the half note, and the quarter note.

The Whole Note

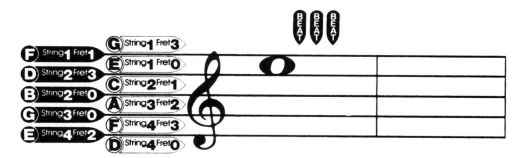

B E A T This symbol represents 1 beat or 1 tap of your foot, (down. up motion of your foot)

1) This E is a whole note. Whole notes are worth **4 beats.** To play this note you strike the 1st string open (no fingers down) and then you count 3 beats. Striking the note is the first beat.

2) O =Whole Note
O =4 beats

Strike Note =1 Beat
+ Count =3 Beats
4 Beats

3) All whole notes are counted the same way. Strike the note and count 3 beats.

4) The **B E A T** symbol will NOT be placed on top of the notes because **the note itself represents 1 beat.** The **beat symbols** will be used as **aides** to **show you how long to pause before proceeding to** the **next note.**

The Half Note

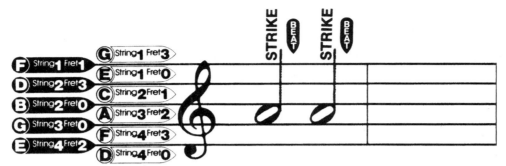

These A's are half notes.
Half notes are worth
2 beats.

1) Strike **A,** or **String 3, Fret 2** and then **count 1 beat after you strike the note.** Striking the note is the first beat.

2) 𝅗𝅥 = Half Note   𝅗𝅥 = 2 Beats

Strike Note = 1 Beat
+ Count = 1 Beat
―――――――
2 Beats

The Quarter Note

Do not count between notes.
Strike each note.

Strike the **D, String 2, Fret 3.**
You proceed from note to note
without counting in-between.

♩ = Quarter Note   ♩ = 1 beat

Strike Note = 1 Beat
+ Count = 0 Beat
―――――――
1 Beat

The best way to read music is to actually do it. Before playing the songs that follow, you should put your hand in the first position.

First Position

1) Putting your hand in the 1st position enables you to play songs without looking at your left hand. **You can't look at the music and your hand at the same time.**

2) Finger and Fret – If your hand is in the first position, when you place your **1st finger** down, you should be on **Fret 1.** When you place your **2nd finger** down, you should be on **Fret 2.** When you place your **3rd finger** down, you should be on **Fret 3.**

3) With your hand in the first position, you won't have to worry about what fret your fingers are on. **Whatever number finger you put down will be the same number fret.**

PLAYING OF SONGS

Directions

1) Most people are very concerned about whether they are playing the correct notes. The simplest and most direct **way of checking** to determine **whether you are playing the correct notes** is by **listening to what you are playing.** The songs chosen in this book are very common tunes that most people are familiar with. This should make checking your notes easier.

2) The first song has only three notes we have discussed: the whole, half, and quarter notes. Remember, you must count as indicated on the music. If there is no counting indicated, proceed to the next note without delay. To create the desired tune you **must stop only when instructed to by the beat symbols** on the music.

3) Listen to the song as you are playing it. If the song doesn't sound the way it should you are either:

1) Playing the wrong note - (check your finger position to **make sure you are on the right fret and striking the right string)** or,

2) Not counting correctly - (**Make sure you are pausing only where you are supposed to.**)

Each song will be presented in two forms. **Form 1** will have a coded staff giving you the position of the note on the neck of the guitar and its name on the staff. The staff will also indicate the count of each note. **Form 2** will present the song in standard musical form.

Form 1
(Coded Staff And Counting Marked In)

This form will give you the opportunity to learn the note's values, names and positions on the neck of the guitar.

Form 2
(Standard Musical Form)

This form will be the same song without any aides marked in. Form 1 should enable you to play songs written in the standard musical form.

The first two songs are made up of notes played entirely on the first three strings of the guitar. All the notes are either whole, half, of quarter notes. In following songs you will use all six strings of the guitar.

Jingle Bells

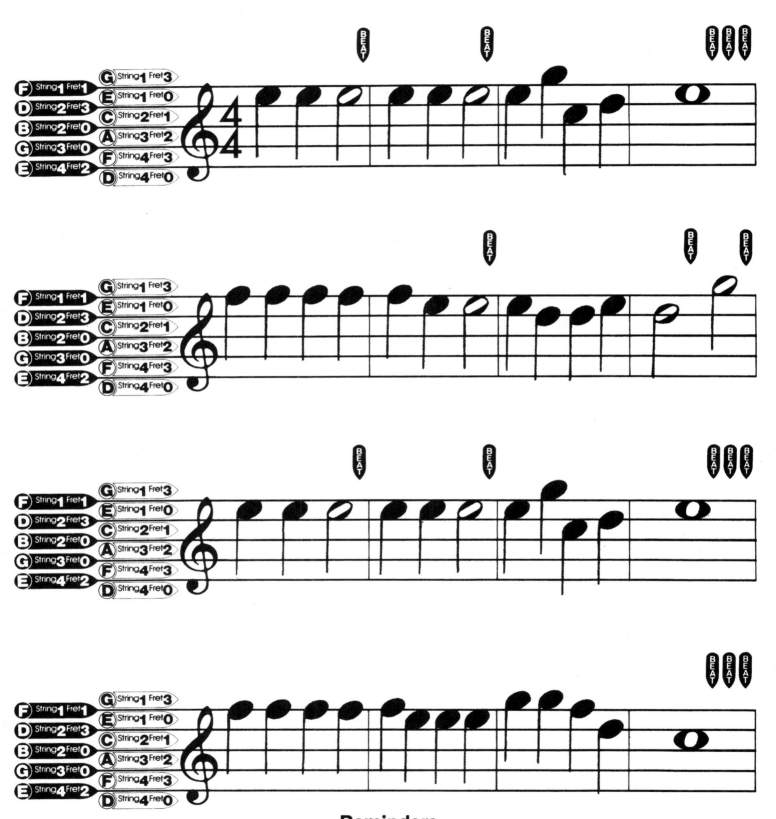

Reminders

1) Begin with your hand in first position.

2) Don't look at your hands. Listen to the tune you are playing and you will know if you are playing the right notes.

Jingle Bells

Can you play the song written in this standard form of music?

Camptown Races

20

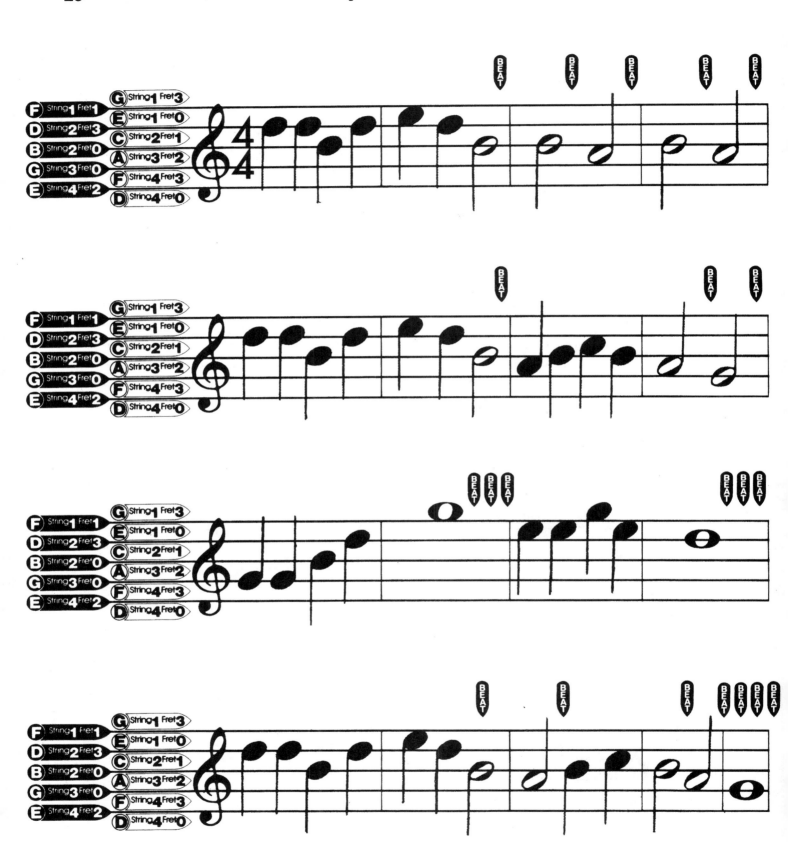

Camptown Races

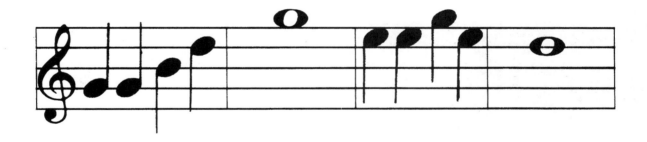

Kum Ba Ya

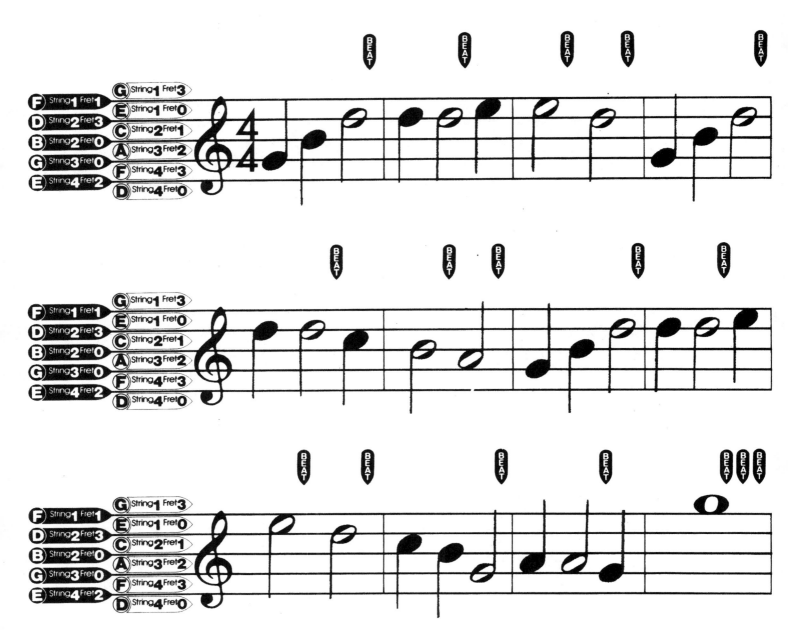

Kum Ba Ya

RESTS

The next song will contain rests and ties. (Ties are explained on the next page.)

1) A rest in music is a period of silence. When you see a rest, count the number of beats it is worth but do not play anything. Each rest symbol indicates how many beats to pause. Three types of rests are shown below.

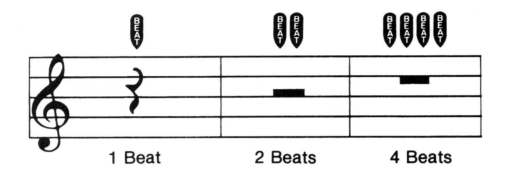

1 Beat   2 Beats   4 Beats

Exercise

Count the value of the note—
then count the value of the rest—

Remember, even though a rest is silent, it is very important that you pause for its **beat** value. A beat is the down, up motion of your foot.

A TIE

1) A tie is when **one note** is **connected** to **another note** with a **looped line.**

2) It does not matter whether the tie is on the top or the bottom of the note.

3) When one note is tied with another note you do not play the second note. Notes that are tied will always be the same notes. When one note is tied to another you play the 1st note and count its value (whole note, half note etc.). **Then you continue to hold the first note** and count the total value of the second note. You count the total value of the second note because you are not playing it. The values of the 2 notes tied will not always be the same.

indicates that you do not play that note but count its value.

Exercise

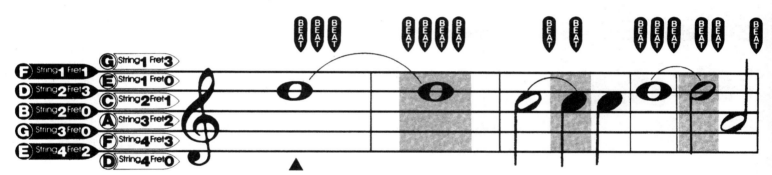

1) Count 3 beats after you strike this note-

2) Count the value of the tie (4 beats) but **do not play the note.**

3) Keep your finger down on **String 2, Fret 3** and let the sound of the note carry on as you count its value and the value of the tie.

The following song will have rests and ties.

TIES AND RESTS

Exercise

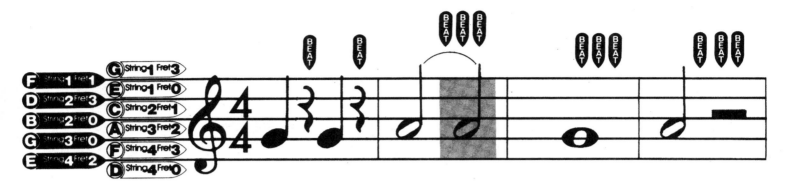

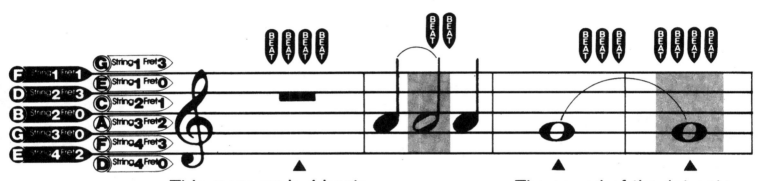

This measure is 4 beats
of silence.

The sound of the 1st note
should carry through as
you count the value of the
tie or second note.

Reminders

Rest - You should count the number of beats needed for a particular rest.

Tie - Play the first note of the tie and let the sound of the first note continue as you
count the value of the second note.

Blank Staff Paper
(Write Your Own Song)

When The Saints Go Marching In

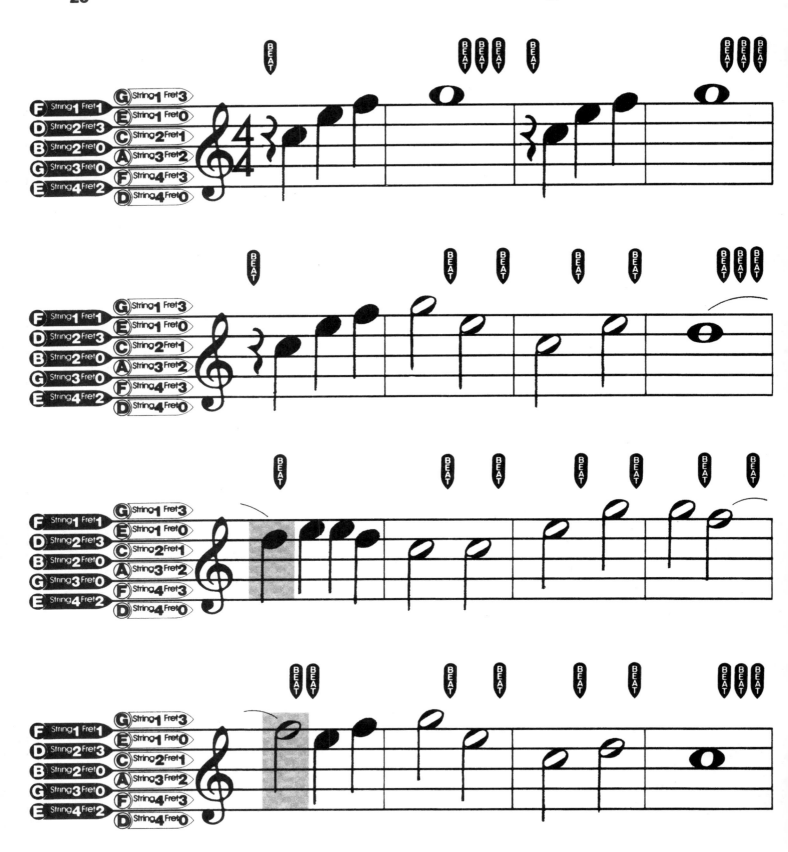

When The Saints Go Marching In

Red River Valley

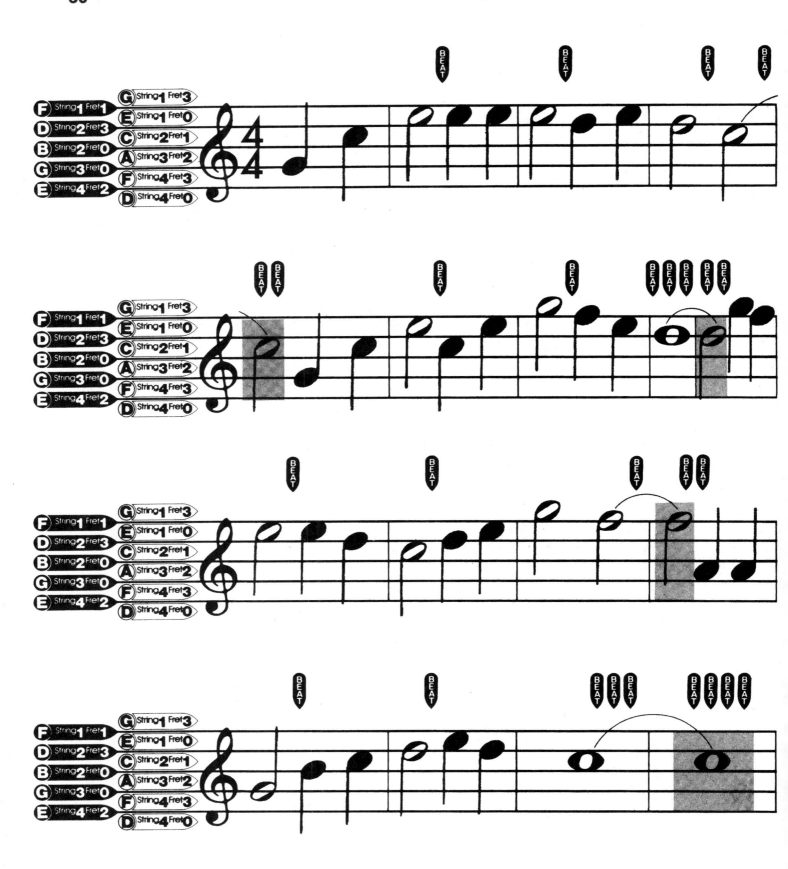

Red River Valley

MORE NOTE VALUES AND COUNTING

The Eighth Note

The next song will contain eighth notes.

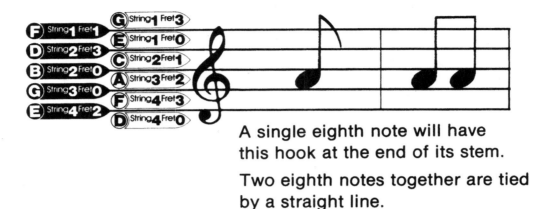

A single eighth note will have this hook at the end of its stem.

Two eighth notes together are tied by a straight line.

1) An eighth note, when it is by itself, will look like ♪ or ♪. When two or more eighth notes are put together they will be connected by a straight line ♫. These are not to be confused by ties. Ties are connected by looped lines. Also unlike notes that are tied, each eighth note is played.

2) An eighth note is worth half a beat. Two eighth notes would equal one quarter note in time. (1 Beat) How do you count a half a beat? Whenever you see an eighth note, speed it up. How much do you speed it up? This is something you must feel. You should play the eighth note twice as fast as a quarter note.

3) Two eighth notes ♪♪ = 1 Beat - two fast strikes equal the pace of one beat.

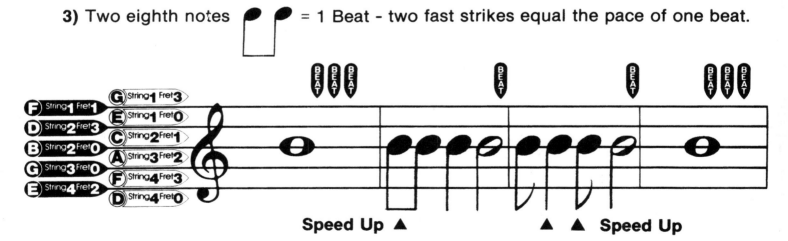

The next song will contain eighth notes. **Two eighth notes** should be **played in** the **down, up motion of your foot.**

Blank Staff Paper
(Write Your Own Song)

Tom Dooley

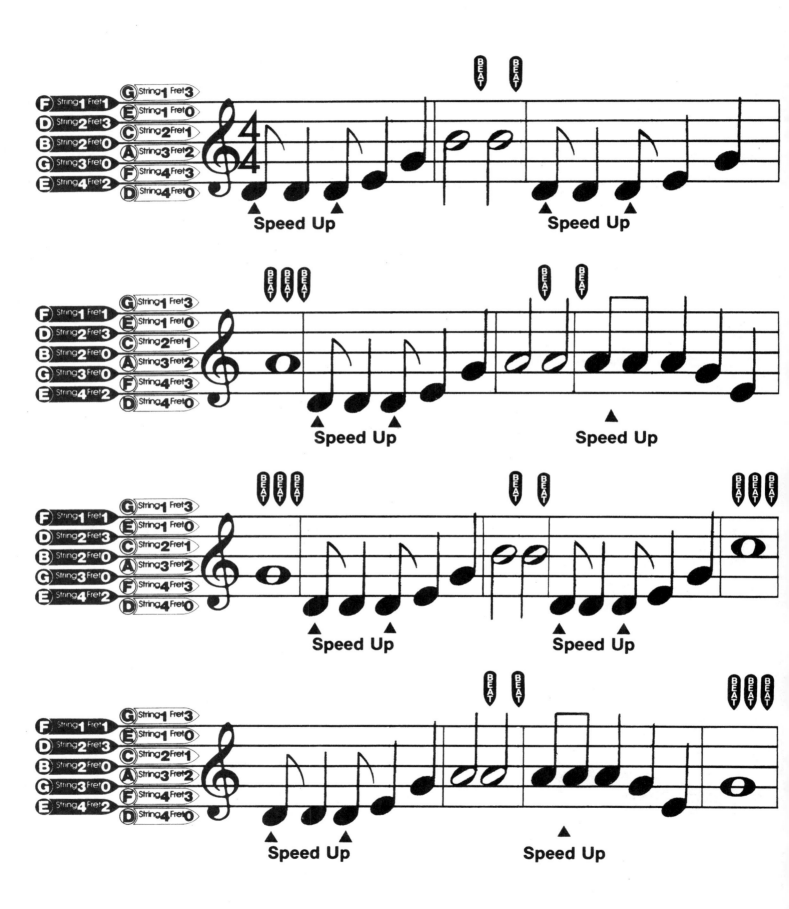

Good Night Ladies

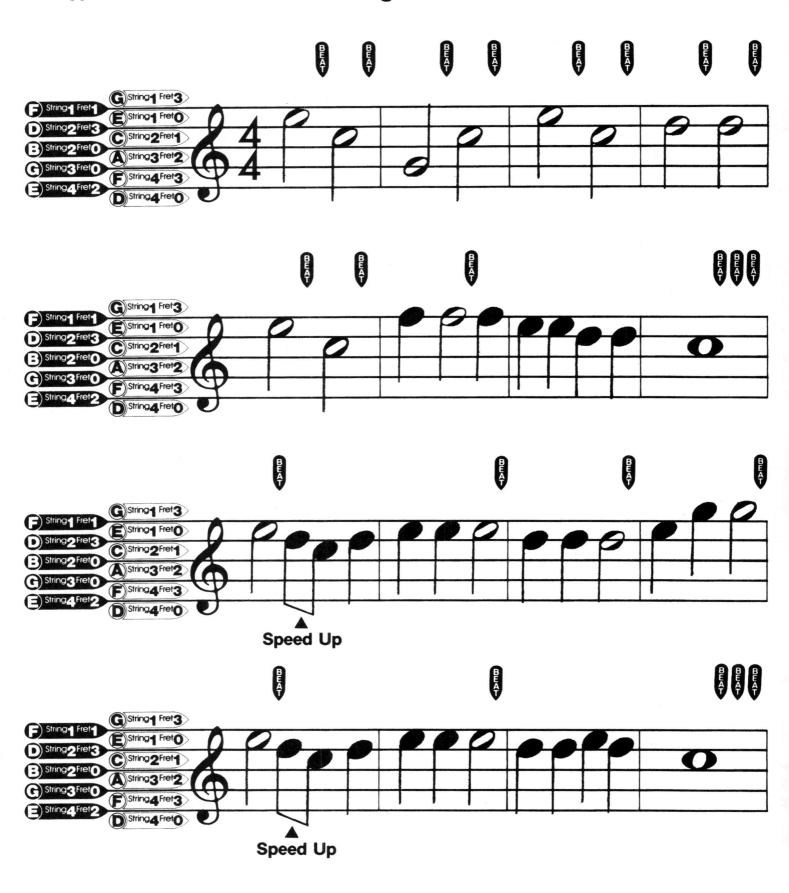

Speed Up

Speed Up

Good Night Ladies

A Dotted Half Note

The next set of songs will contain dotted half notes and dotted quarter notes (Dotted quarter notes are explained on the next page.)

These are **dotted half notes. They are worth 3 beats.** Strike the note and then count 2 beats. Striking the note is the 1st beat.

𝅗𝅥• = Dotted Half Note   𝅗𝅥• = 3 Beats

Strike Note = 1 Beat
+ Count = <u>2 Beats</u>
3 Beats

Exercise

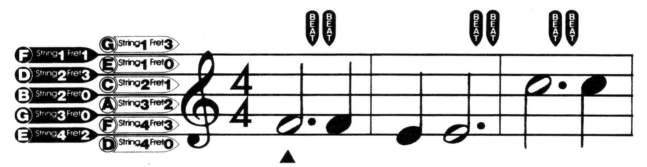

▲
Strike the note -
Count the beats and proceed.

Student Notes

A Dotted Quarter Note

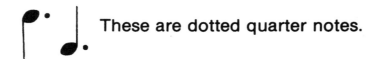 These are dotted quarter notes.

1) A dotted quarter note is worth 1½ Beats.

♩• = dotted quarter note   ♩• = 1½ Beats

Strike note = 1 Beat
+ Count = ½ Beat (say "and")
1½ Beats

2) How do you count half a beat? We learned with eighth notes to count half a beat. However, you say "and" after you play the note. In other words, there is a slight pause or hesitation before you play the next note. A dotted quarter note is usually preceded or followed by an eighth note.

Exercise

Reminders

A dotted quarter note is almost always followed by an eighth note. You should be able to play both notes in two taps of your foot. Playing both notes takes 2 beats.

Auld Lang Syne

40

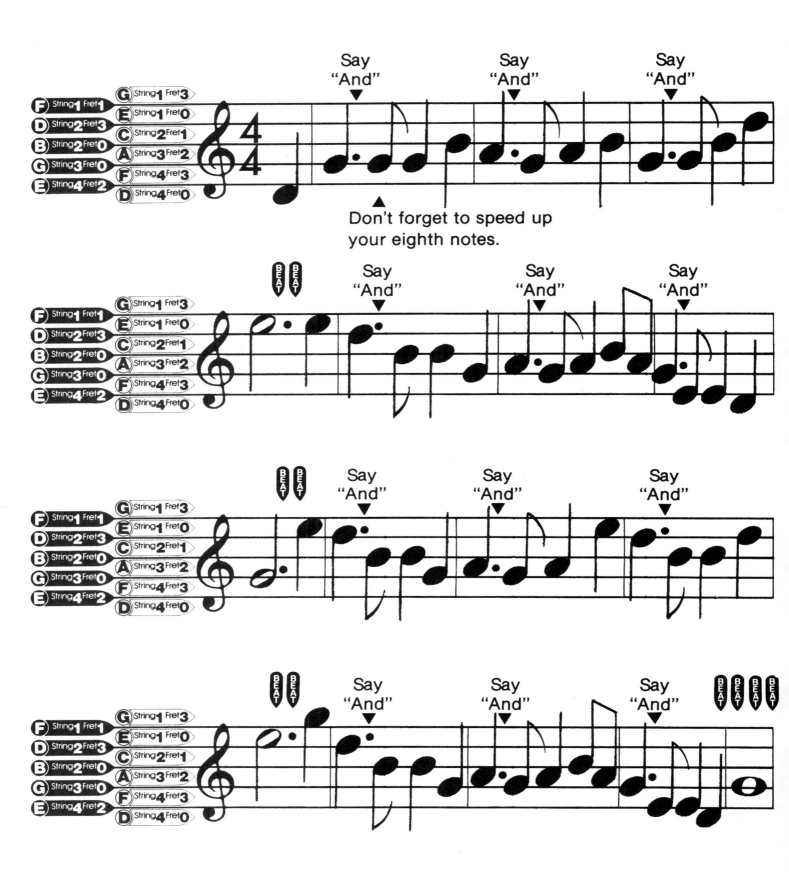

Don't forget to speed up
your eighth notes.

Auld Lang Syne

On Top Of Old Smokey

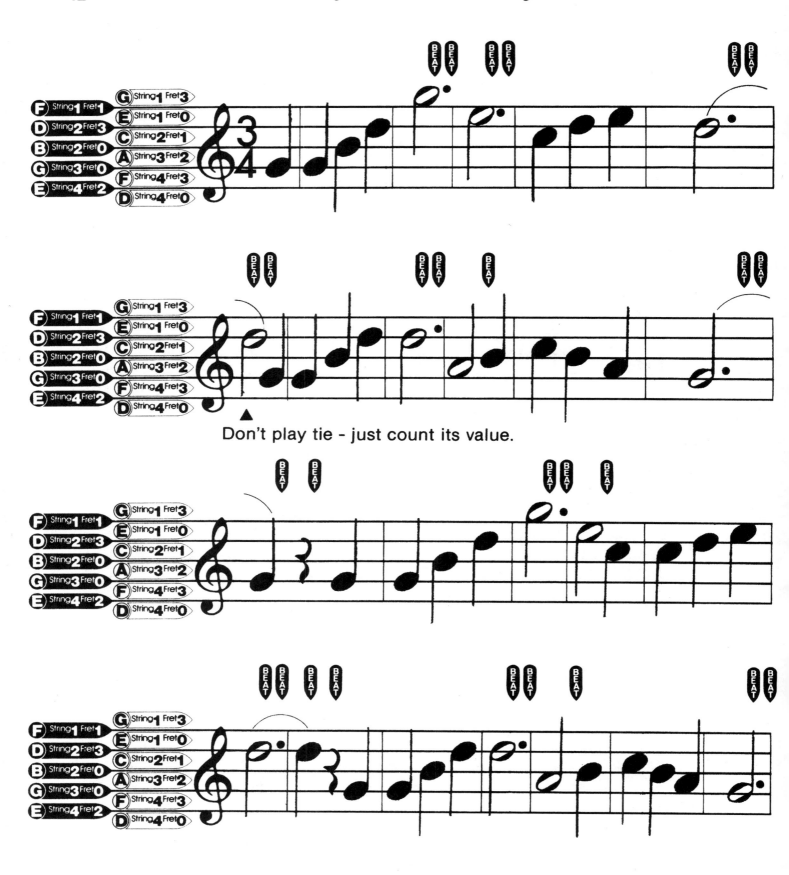

Don't play tie - just count its value.

On Top Of Old Smokey

Oh Susanna

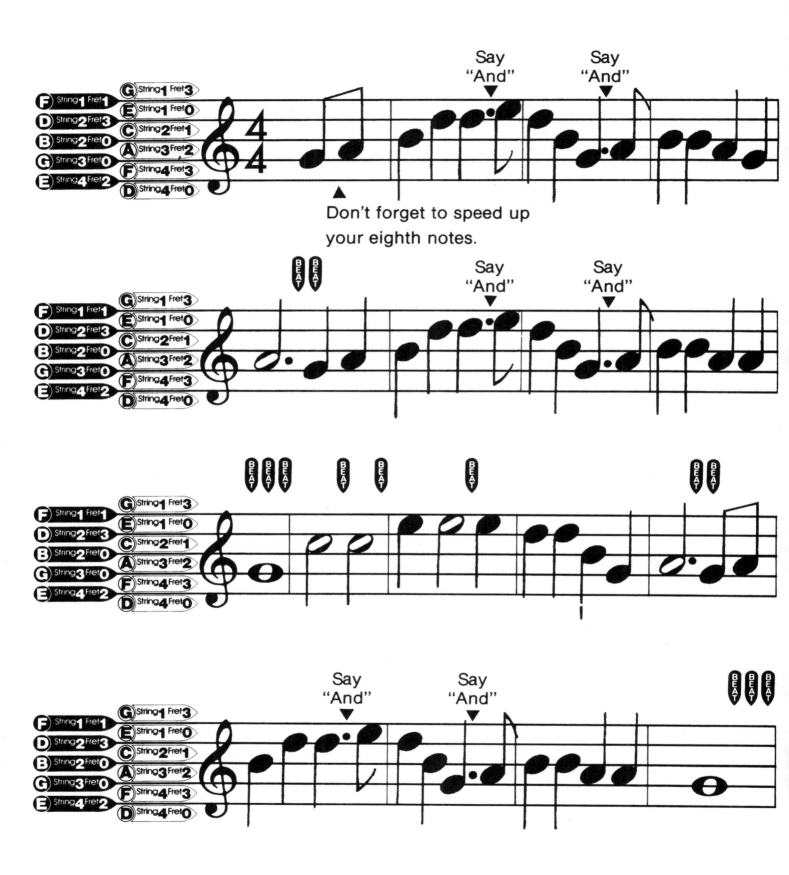

Don't forget to speed up
your eighth notes.

Oh Susanna

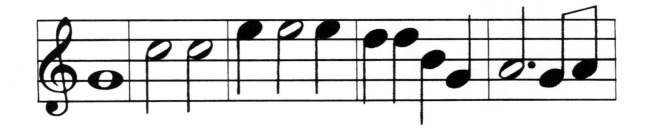

THE FIFTH AND SIXTH STRINGS

Up until now you have been given songs which can be played entirely on the first four strings of the guitar. As noted earlier, a standard staff is composed of 5 lines and 4 spaces. The first four strings of the guitar take up the entire standard staff. The staff and first four strings are shown below.

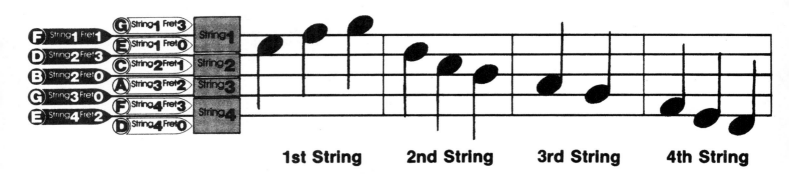

The **notes** for the **5th** and **6th strings** are **placed below** the **standard staff.** The lines and spaces of the staff are extended below the standard staff in order to accommodate the 5th and 6th strings. The notes representing the 5th and 6th strings are shown on the following page.

Student Notes

_____

The 5th String

The notes for the 5th String are placed on extended lines and spaces of the standard staff.

The 6th String

The notes for the 6th string are also placed on extended lines and spaces of the staff.

Naming The Notes Below The Staff

The lines and spaces are in alphabetical order. Remember, the musical alphabet stops at **G** and begins again at **A. A, B, C, D, E, F, G, A, B, C,** etc. The note takes on the name of the line or space that it is on.

The following songs have notes which are played on the 5th and 6th strings of the guitar.

COUNTING AND NOTE VALUE REVIEW

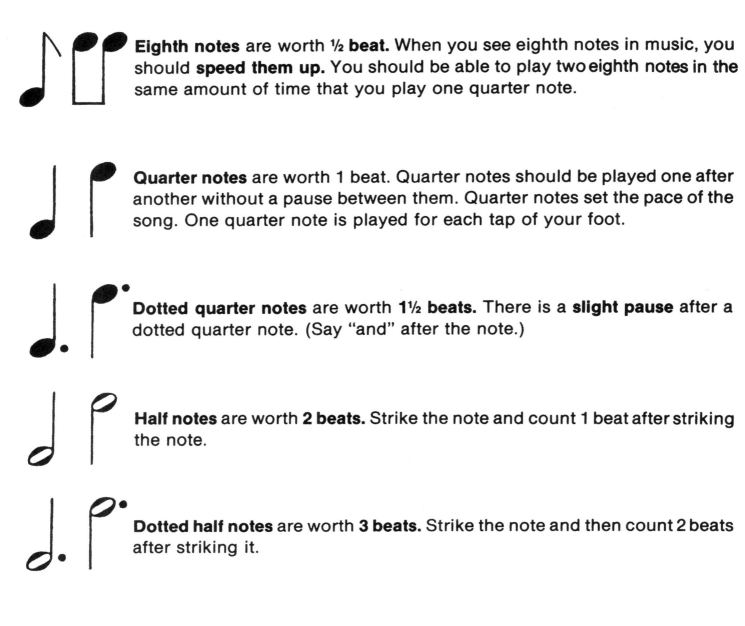

Eighth notes are worth ½ **beat.** When you see eighth notes in music, you should **speed them up.** You should be able to play two eighth notes in the same amount of time that you play one quarter note.

Quarter notes are worth 1 beat. Quarter notes should be played one after another without a pause between them. Quarter notes set the pace of the song. One quarter note is played for each tap of your foot.

Dotted quarter notes are worth 1½ beats. There is a **slight pause** after a dotted quarter note. (Say "and" after the note.)

Half notes are worth **2 beats.** Strike the note and count 1 beat after striking the note.

Dotted half notes are worth **3 beats.** Strike the note and then count 2 beats after striking it.

Whole notes are worth **4 beats.** Strike the note and then count 3 beats after striking it. Striking the note is the 1st beat.

Blank Staff Paper
(Write Your Own Song)

Shoo Fly, Don't Bother Me

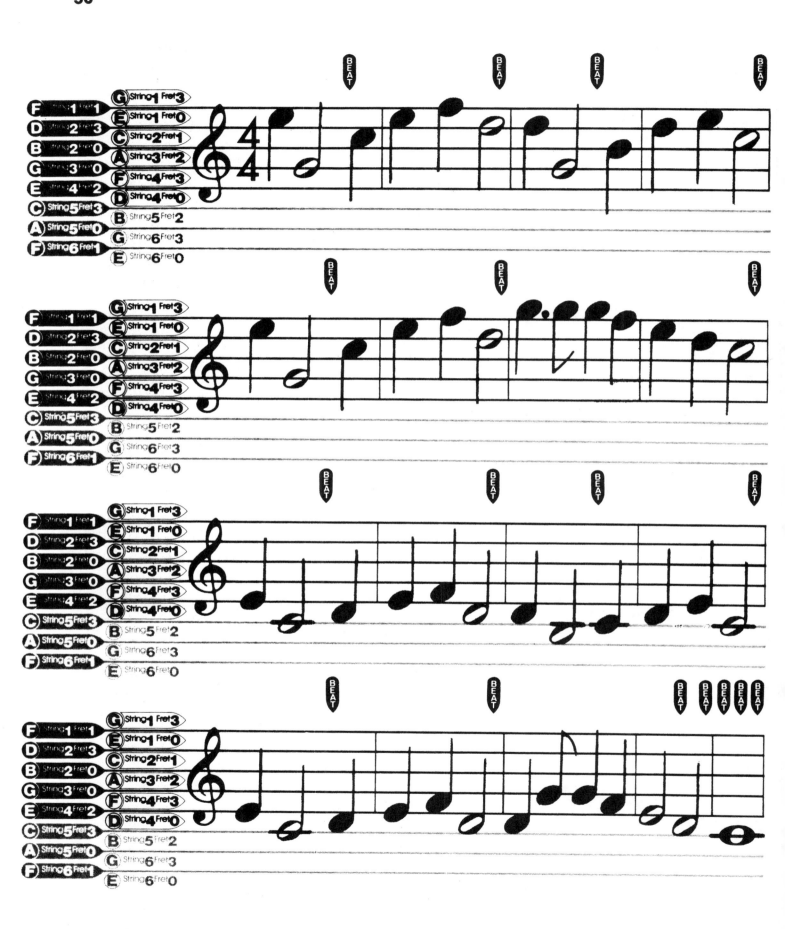

Shoo Fly, Don't Bother Me

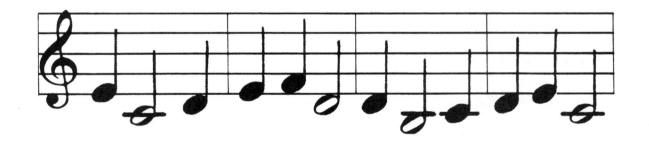

Scarborough Fair

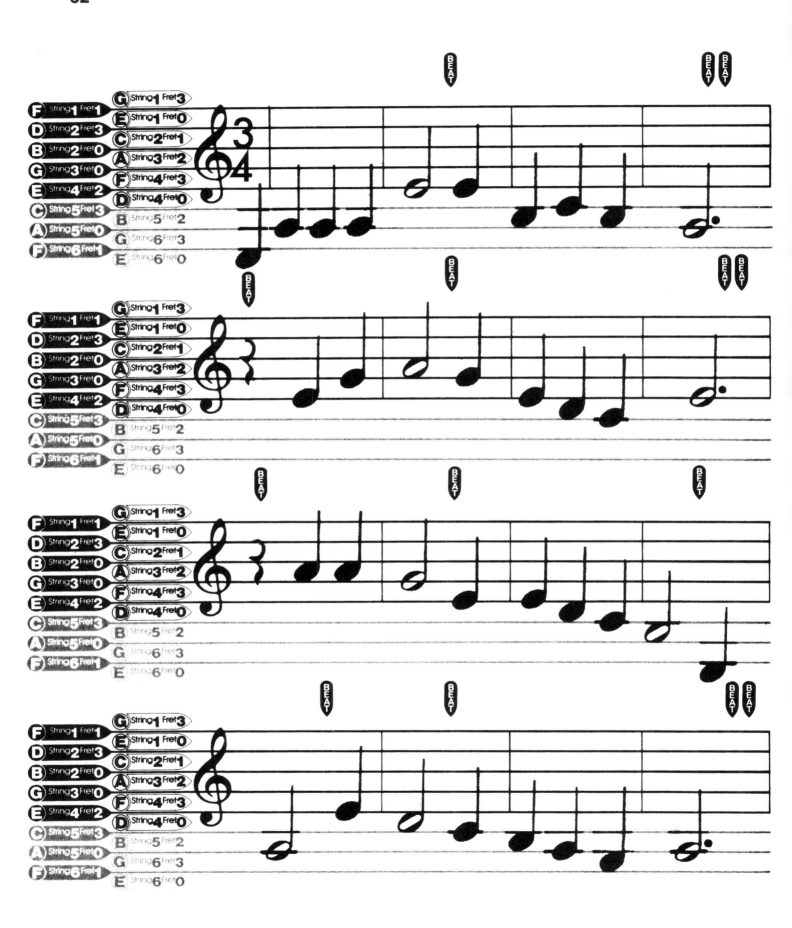

Scarborough Fair

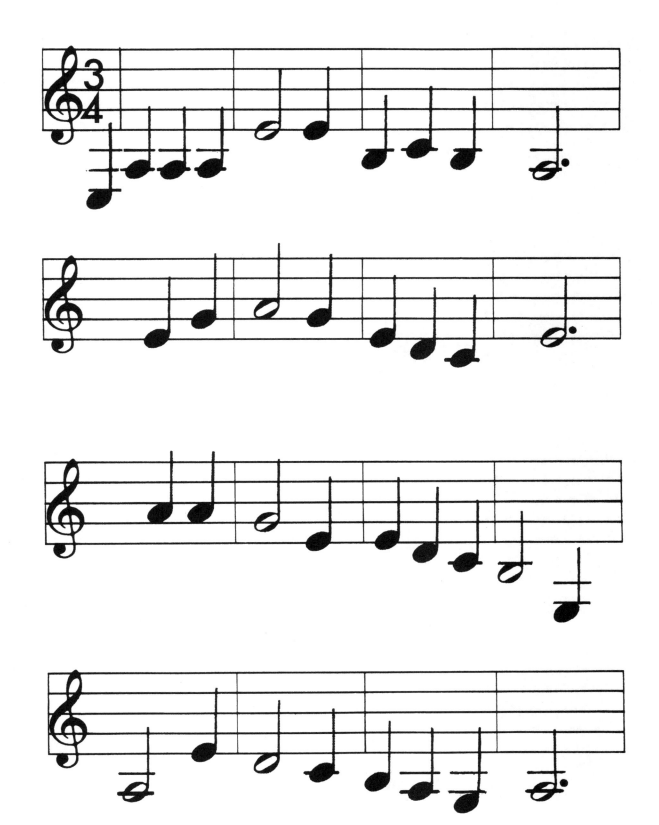

I've Been Working On The Railroad

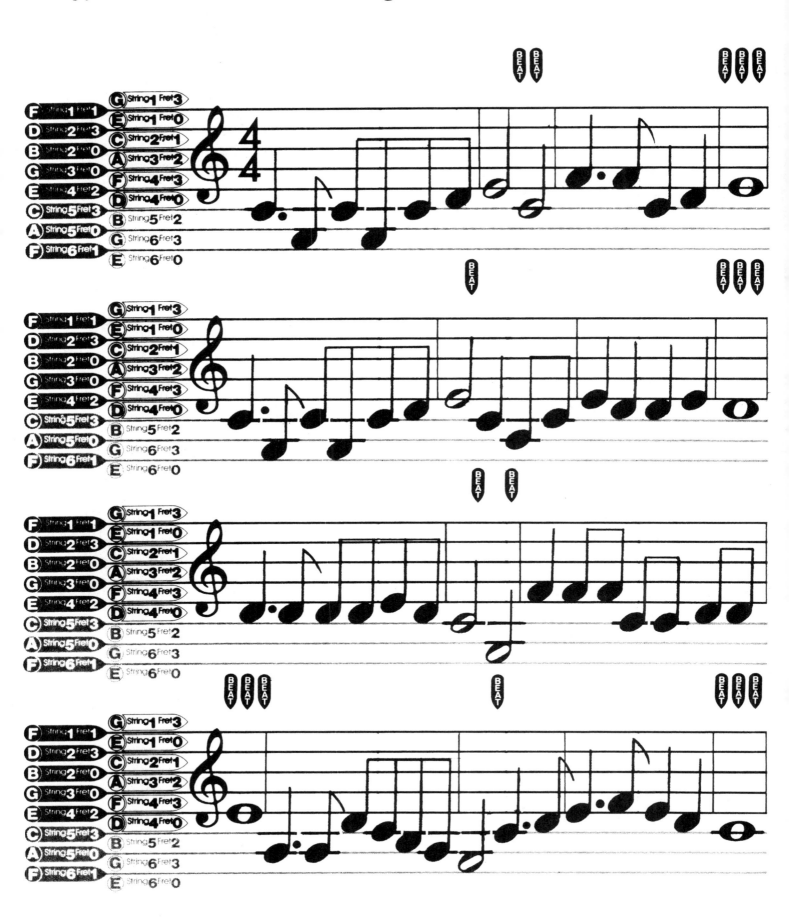

I've Been Working On The Railroad

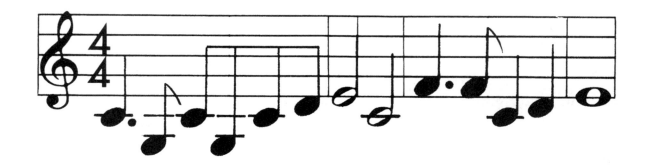

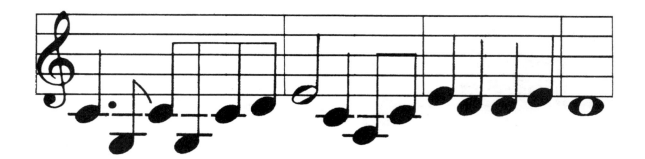

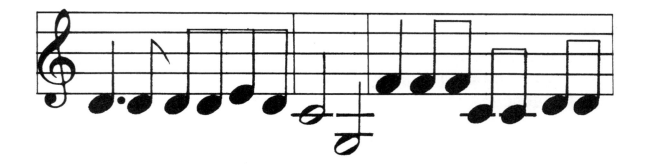

SHARPS ♯

In this section we will discuss the general rules of sharps and what affect they will have on the position of notes on the neck of the guitar.

General Rules

1) This is a sharp sign ♯

2) When you see this sign you must do something to the note it affects.

3) The sharp sign will appear in two different ways on the music.

A. The sharp sign always appears on the left of the note it affects. Once a sharp appears in front of a note you must **sharp the rest of the notes in that measure with the same name.**

This A would be sharp

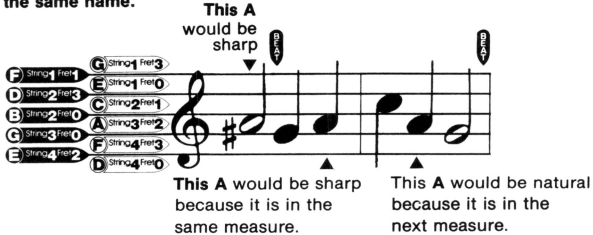

This **A** would be sharp because it is in the same measure.

This **A** would be natural because it is in the next measure.

B. The sharp sign may also appear in the key signature or the very beginning of song. When the sharp sign appears before the time signature, all the notes of the line or space of the staff it is on will be sharp.

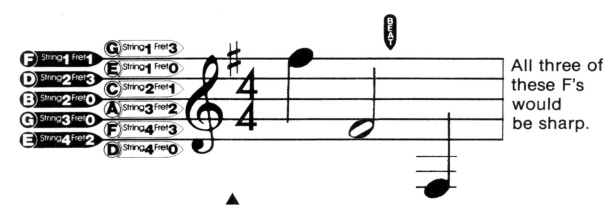

All three of these F's would be sharp.

As you can see, the sharp sign is on the **F** line of the staff. This means that **all F's** in this song would be sharp.

SHARPS ♯

Number 1

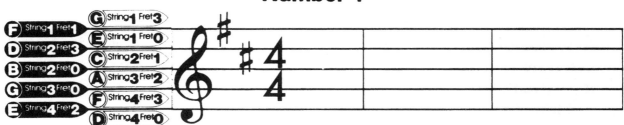

1) In song **number 1** all F's would be sharp because the sharp sign is on the F line of the staff. Also, in this song, all C's would be sharp because the sharp sign is on the C space of the staff. **Remember, the only notes that are affected in this song would be F and C. All other notes would be played in their regular or natural way.** A song does not have to have sharp signs in the beginning, but it may.

Number 2

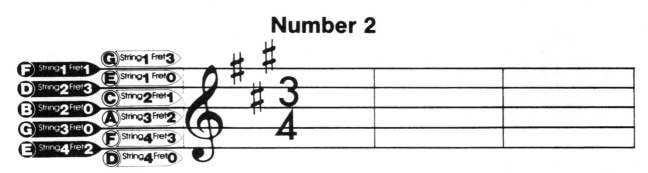

2) In song **number 2** all C's would be sharp becase the sharp sign is on the C space. Also, in this song, all G's would be sharp because the sharp sign is on the G space. All F's would be sharp because the sharp sign is on the F line.

3) Before you play any song you should check for sharp signs. If a note is supposed to be sharp and you don't sharp it, the tune will sound incorrect.

HOW TO SHARP A NOTE

General Rule

To sharp a note on the guitar you move the note up one fret (towards the hole in your guitar) and remain on the same string. The position of the natural note will be enclosed in a circle and the sharped note will be shaded. This rule applies to all notes for the guitar. (Example follows)

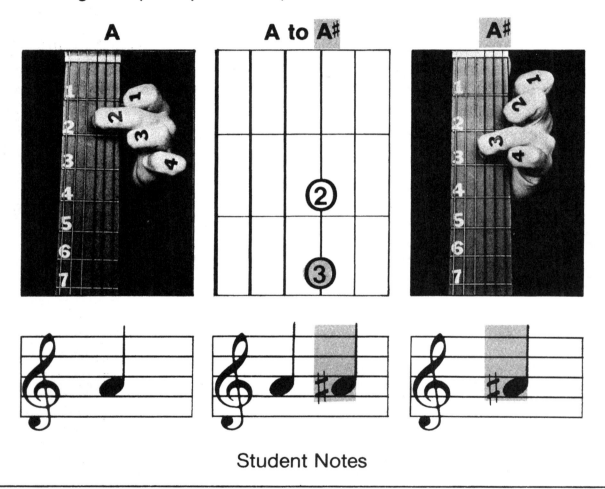

Student Notes

General Rule

To sharp an open string you play **Fret 1** of the string that is to be sharped.(Example follows) The position of the sharped note will be enclosed in a circle. An open string is playing a string of your guitar with no fingers down on your left hand.

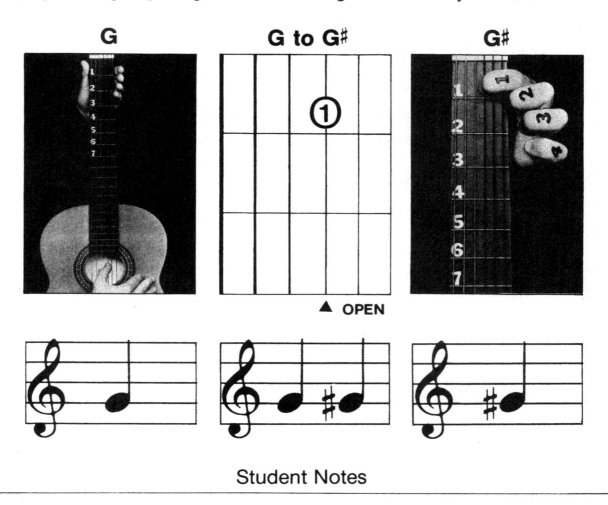

Student Notes

THE NATURAL SIGN ♮

The natural sign removes the sharp.

Example 1

This F would also be natural because it is in the same measure.

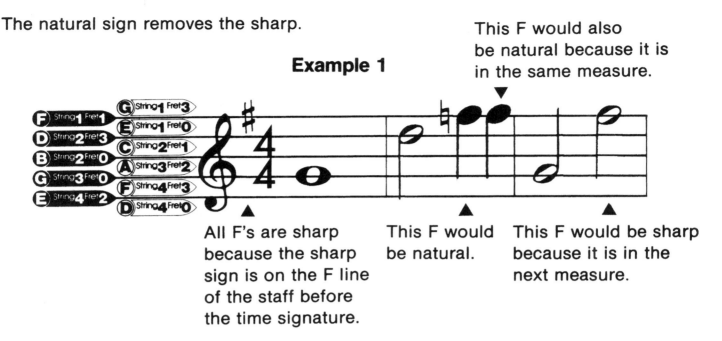

All F's are sharp because the sharp sign is on the F line of the staff before the time signature.

This F would be natural.

This F would be sharp because it is in the next measure.

In this piece of music F's would be sharp. The F that has the natural sign before it would be played on String 1, Fret 1, just like a regular F. The F that follows in the next measure would be sharp again. **The natural sign removes the sharp from that one particular F and all other F's in that measure, if there are any.**

Example 2

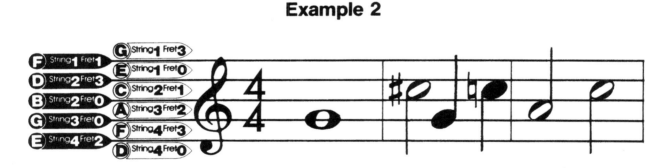

In this example C was made sharp. The rest of the C's that follow in that measure would also be sharp. Once the natural sign is placed on the C, the remainder of the C's in that measure would be ordinary C (1st finger, String 2, Fret 1) unless another sharp sign is placed down.

The following songs will give you some practice using sharps on the guitar.

Blank Staff Paper
(Write Your Own Song)

Give Me That Old Time Religion

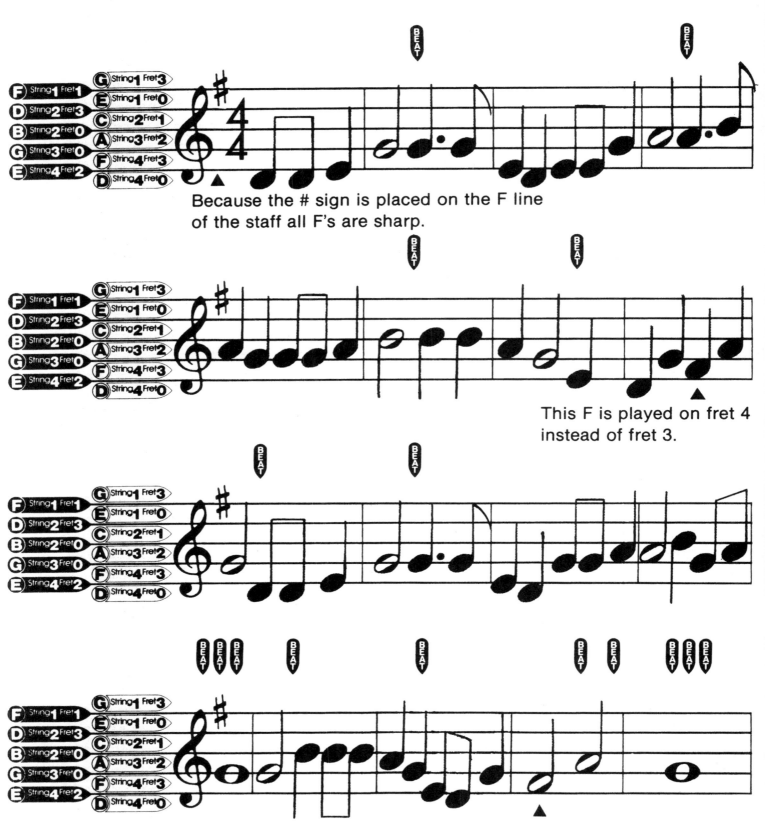

Because the # sign is placed on the F line
of the staff all F's are sharp.

This F is played on fret 4
instead of fret 3.

This F is played on string 4, fret 4
instead of string 4, fret 3.

Give Me That Old Time Religion

Beautiful Dreamer

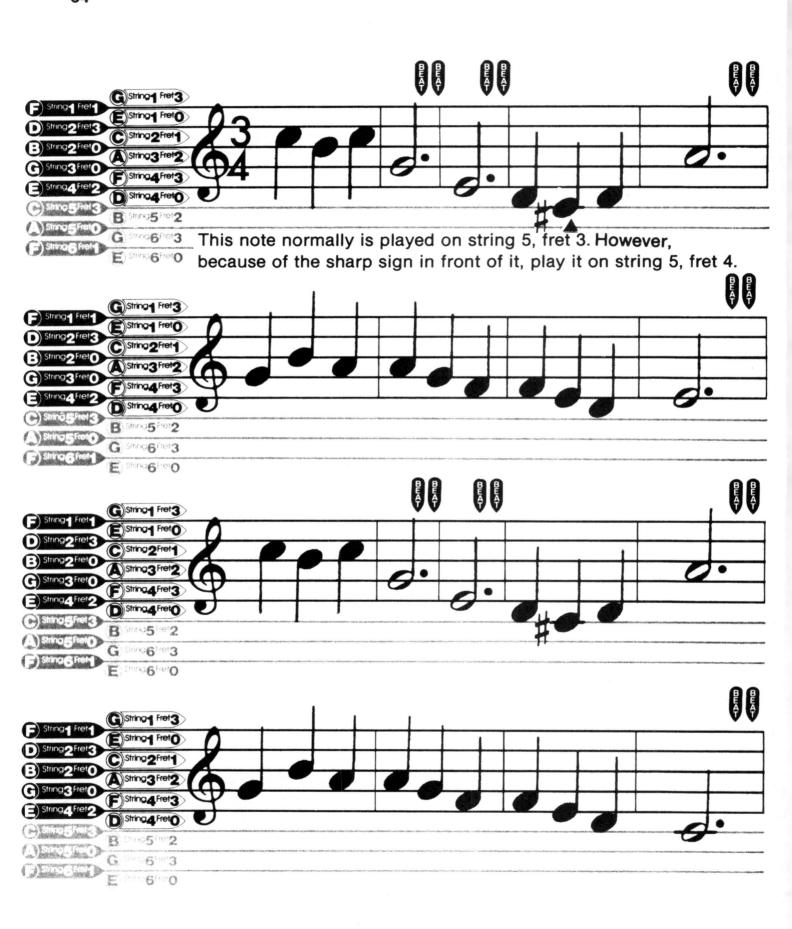

This note normally is played on string 5, fret 3. However, because of the sharp sign in front of it, play it on string 5, fret 4.

Beautiful Dreamer

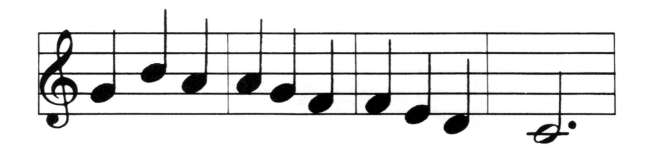

Home On The Range

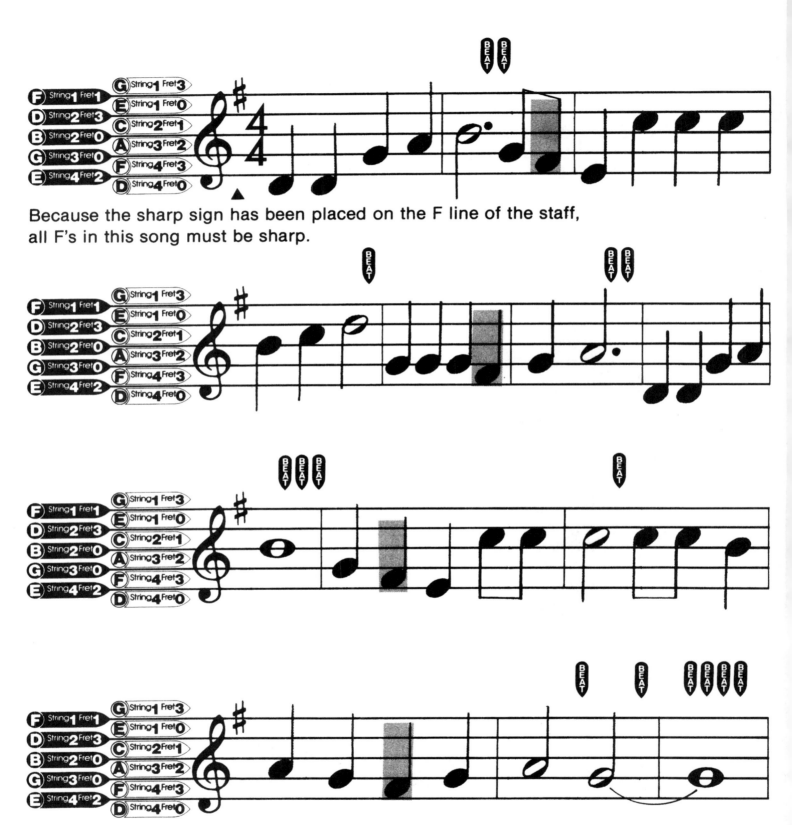

Because the sharp sign has been placed on the F line of the staff,
all F's in this song must be sharp.

All the F's have been indicated with shading and are played on string 4, fret 4, rather
than string 4, fret 3.

Home On The Range

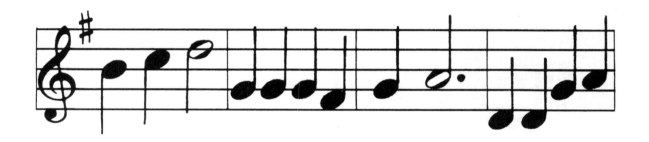

FLATS ♭

General Rules

1) This is a flat sign ♭

2) When you see this sign you must do something to the note it affects.

3) The flat sign will appear in two different ways on the music.

A. The flat sign always appears to the left of the note it affects. **Once a flat sign appears on a note you must flat that note and the rest ot the notes in that measure.**

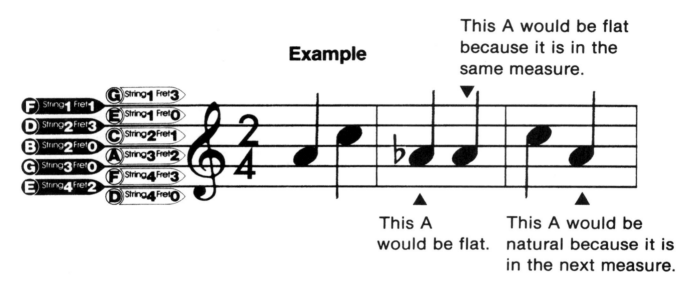

Example

This A would be flat because it is in the same measure.

This A would be flat.

This A would be natural because it is in the next measure.

Student Notes

B. The flat sign may also appear in the key signature or the very beginning of the song.

All B's would be flat in this song
because the flat sign is on the B line
of the staff before the time signature
of the song.

4) As you can see the flat sign is on the B line of the staff. This means that all B's in this song will be flat. All other notes would be played in their regular or natural way.

Both of these B's, as well
as any other B in this song,
would have to be flat.

5) In this piece all E's would be flat and all B's would be flat. The flat sign is on the E space of the staff and is also on the B line of the staff. The only notes in this song that would be affected are E's and B's.

HOW TO FLAT A NOTE

General Rule

To flat a note on the guitar you must move the note down one fret (towards the top of the guitar) and stay on the same string. (Example follows) The position of the natural notes will be enclosed in a circle and the flatted notes will be shaded. This rule applies to all flatted notes except open strings, which are explained on the next page.

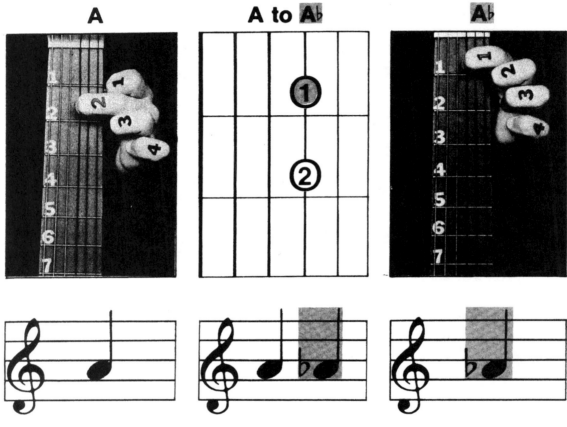

A   **A to A♭**   **A♭**

Student Notes

General Rule

To **flat** an **open string** you move to the **next string** and **play Fret 4**. If **String 1, Open** is flat you move to **String 2, Fret 4**. If **String 3, Open** is flat you would move to **String 4, Fret 4,** etc. An example follows. See exception next page.

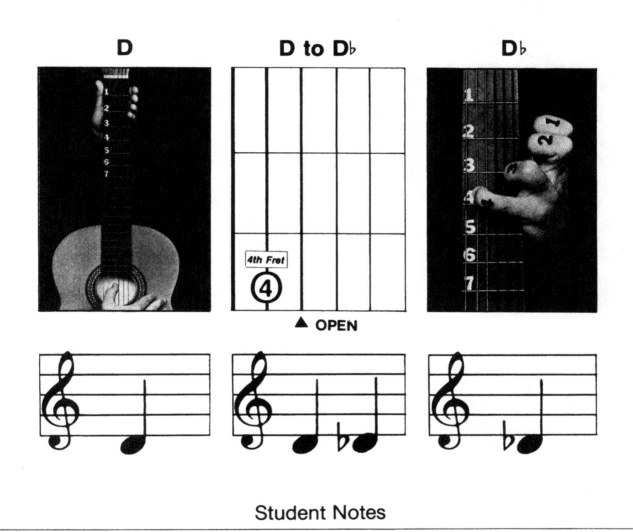

D　　　　**D to D♭**　　　　**D♭**

4th Fret ④

▲ OPEN

Student Notes

FLATS - EXCEPTIONS TO THE RULE

Exception 1

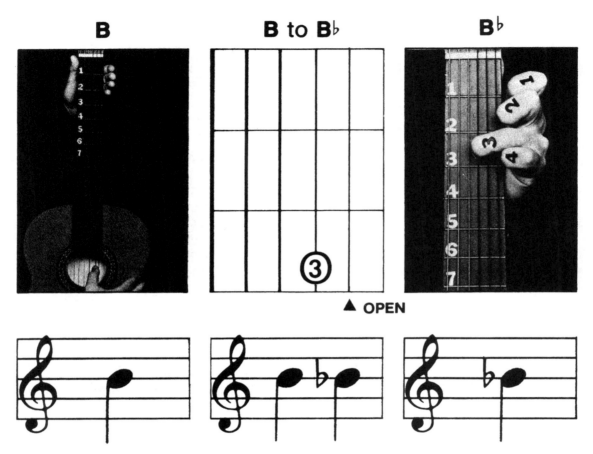

B   **B to B♭**   **B♭**

▲ OPEN

As you can see, the open **B** is moved to the **next string, (String 3), Fret 3,** rather than **Fret 4** like the other open strings.

Exception 2

F and **C** and **F** are on **Fret 1.** so to flat them you must play that string open.

You cannot play this note - it is out of range.

1) The natural sign removes the flat from a note.

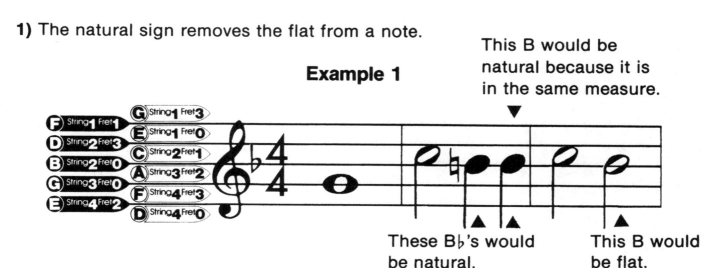

Example 1

This B would be natural because it is in the same measure.

These B♭'s would be natural.

This B would be flat.

In this piece of music all B's would be flat. The exception would be the B that has the natural sign. This B would be played like a regular B (String 2, Open). The B that follows in the same measure would also be natural. The B that follows in the next measure should be made flat again.

Example 2

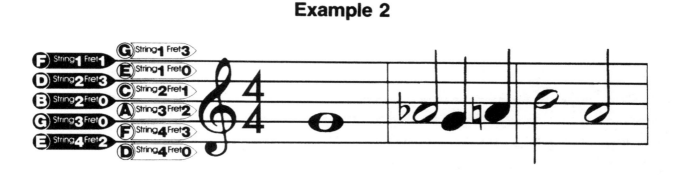

In this example, A was made flat and the rest of the A's that follow in that measure would also have to be made flat. Once the natural sign is placed on the A, the remainder of the A's in that measure would be regular A. (2nd finger, String 3, Fret 2)

Clementine

Because this ♭ (flat) sign is placed on the B line of the staff, all B's in this song are flat.

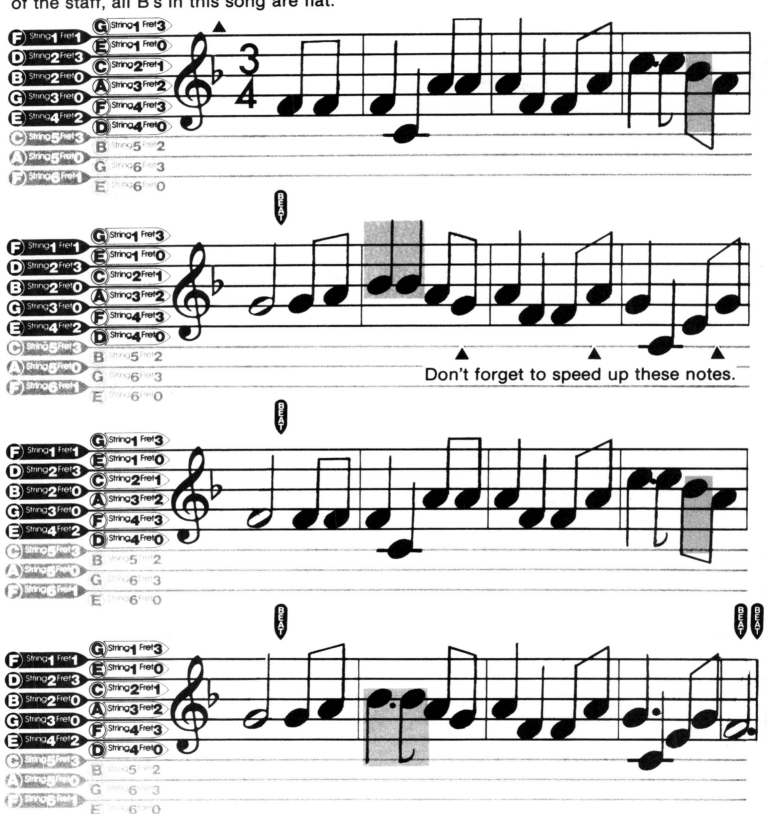

Don't forget to speed up these notes.

All the B's in this song have been shaded and must be flatted. Because they are flat you would play them on string 3, fret 3, rather than string 2, open.

Clementine

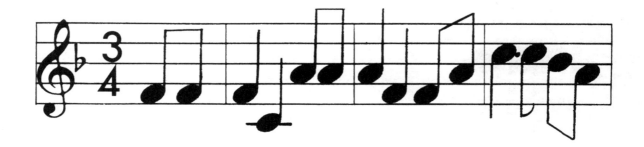

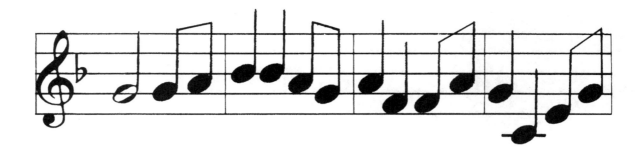

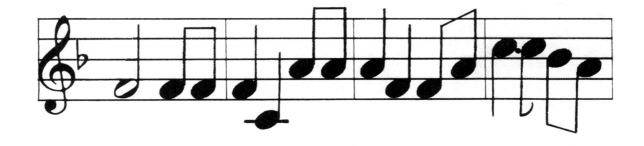

Swanee River

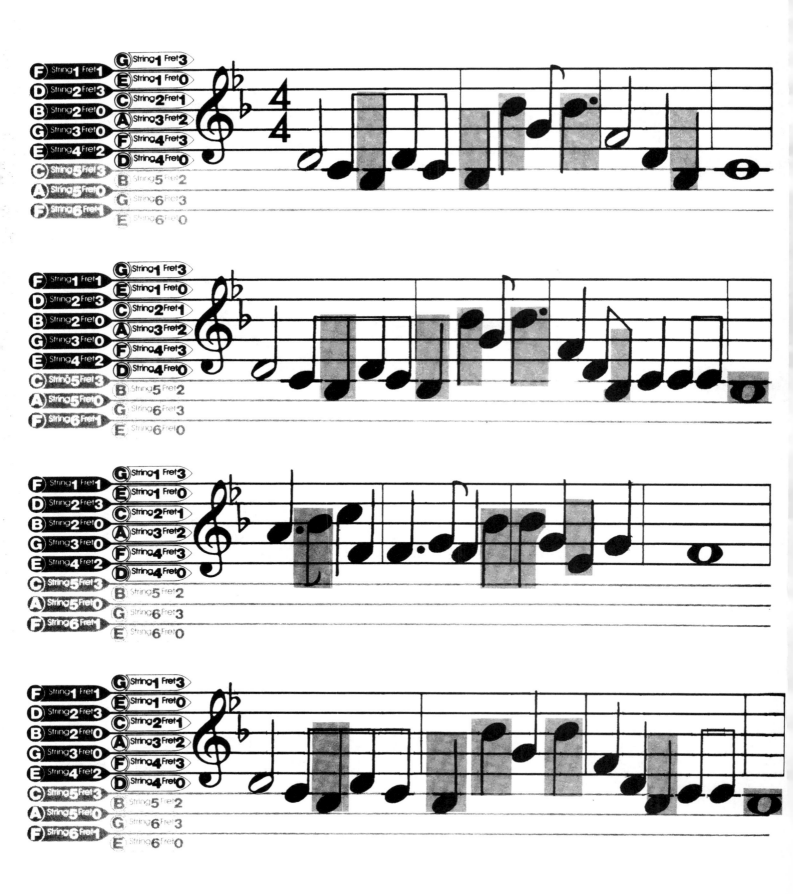

Swanee River

There are two flats in the key signature of Swanee River. All flat notes have been shaded. How to flat is shown below.

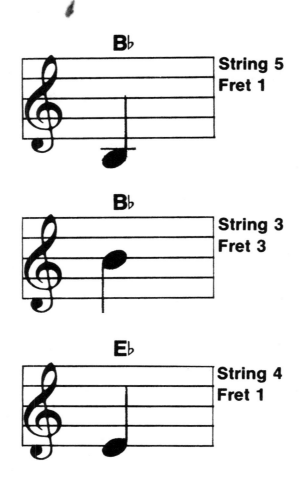

B♭
String 5
Fret 1

B♭
String 3
Fret 3

E♭
String 4
Fret 1

Conclusion

Always remember to check the key signature for sharps and flats before you begin the song. If there are sharp or flat signs in the key signature, you must sharp or flat the notes affected.